God Has Our Backs
Making Sense of the Bible for Teens

Written and Illustrated by
R. Cherie Lepeak

James Kay Publishing

Tulsa, Oklahoma

God Has Our Backs

Making Sense of the Bible for Teens

ISBN 978-1-943245-65-9

www.jameskaypublishing.com

e-mail: sales@jameskaypublishing.com

© 2021 Cherie Lepeak
Gover Art by Ethan and Noah Buechler
Author Photo by Steven Lepeak

1.1

A Note From The Author

It all started forty years ago, I was twenty-two then. I watched my parents struggling to get their homework done as they attended the Bristol Road School of Biblical Studies in Flint Michigan. I was a young mother of two and although I was very proud of their undertaking, I just wanted their attention on my little ones instead of their noses in their studies.

After my parents graduated from the school, it wasn't until years later that I felt the full impact of what they had learned.

My Dad preached and later became and elder of the Church. My Mother used her knowledge to be a ladies' Bible class teacher. But the things they were teaching were different and amazing! I'd never heard the Bible taught with such clarity! It was very exciting to me as I sat in my Mother's class.

Soon after our lessons were concluded, one of the elder's wives approached my Mother and said she had never heard anything like this taught before. She said it opened her eyes about the Bible being one story with one plan. She then proceeded to tell my mother she should write her lessons in a book form so others could pass on what she was teaching.

That started the ball rolling. One of my sisters, Kellie, and I worked side-by-side with my mother for about a year. We typed, gathered her illustrations, and continued to type until finally her class study book was created! The title is *Redemption Through Jesus, Planned, Prophesied and Fulfilled* by Rita G. Draper. Since then her book has been taught in many classrooms all across the country.

A few years later, I volunteered to teach our ladies' Bible class and decided to teach my Mother's book. I was scared as I had only taught children before. But as I taught, our preacher's wife told me she had never heard teaching like this before. She said it made the Bible so understandable and gave purpose to all the Old Testament stories connecting them to the New Testament as one story! She was so excited!

Soon after I finished teaching the ladies' Bible class on Tuesdays, I took my turn teaching our Sunday morning Children's class. Because we were a small congregation, I taught ages five through eleven. It was a challenge, but I love challenges! As I thought about what to teach the children, I decided to teach them what the ladies were learning only on a children's level. That was the start of my first book entitled, *The Wonderful Story of God's Plan for Jesus.* (Coming Soon) As I wrote and needed specific illustrations, I just created my own. Everyone got such a kick out of my art work!

When I finished that book, I read it to a few of my older grandchildren. They loved it and asked if I could write another book for teenagers. I said, "Of course!" and started writing my second book, *God Has our Backs, Making Sense of the Bible for Teens.*

After I finished, I met with my grandchildren again. We read through a couple chapters a week until we made it through to the end. They applauded and loved it! They were such an encouragement to me!

My desire is to teach young people the things I never knew as a young Christian. Two of the things being the blessing of knowing the Bible as one complete story and the assurance of having a home with God forever when we die.

While reading this book, there may be subject matter that raises questions in your minds. Feel free to ask as many questions as you need. Make sure you ask a person you trust as a good Bible mentor.

In fact, at the end of each chapter, I have asked a few questions as a "Knowledge Check." In the back of the book is the "Answer Key to the Knowledge Check" questions.

I have written out the verses from the Bible I used throughout my book. Unless otherwise stated, they have all come from the *New International Version*. Other versions I used were the *Contemporary English Version, English Standard Version, New American Standard Version,* and *The Passion Translation*.

I know you will love reading this book, giving it as a gift, or sharing it with friends or neighbors. Give hope in this world to someone you love!

In Christian Love,

With all my heart,

R. Cherie Lepeak

Contents

Acknowledgements

This book was written with the hope of furthering the
message of the Bible to all of our youth. Even though targeting
teenagers, this book is great reading for all ages. It will take you through
the entire Bible making It as the one story It was written to be.
After Reading each chapter there is a section called "Knowledge Check".
See how many of the questions you can answer.

My mother, Rita Draper, wrote the book these chapters originated from.
Her book entitled *Redemption through Christ, Planned, Prophesied and Fulfilled*
was written for fifth grade through adult ages to be used as class material.
Her book has been taught in many classrooms across our country.

Thank you to my Daddy, Garland Draper and Mama, Rita, for being such a
great Christian example and raising me to know our wonderful God.
Thank you to my husband, Steve, for being supportive and
patient while I worked writing and illustrating this book.
I wish to thank our children,
Chrissy, Aron, Mike, Amanda, Patrick, Megan,
Kari, Joe, and Steven for helping to inspire this work.

I also wish to thank our grandchildren for their inspiration and
sharing their wonderful art work used in my book. Their artwork is listed in
the contents by the name and age of the child who created it.

Thanks to my sister, Gwen, for her help and patience along with
my sister, Kellie, for all of their support.

Most of all, I wish to thank God for making His plan
to bring Jesus to save us from our sins!

In Christian Love, R. Cherie Lepeak

"The Tree" By Colette

Chapter 1

In all of our lives, being in our teen years can sometimes be the most confusing, frustrating, and crazy time we ever experience. While at the same time it can be the most free, exciting, and fun-loving time ever!

We question everything from authority to our very existence. As teenagers, we are always searching to fill an empty spot in our hearts or minds. Sometimes we try to fill it with things, friends, or love. Only to either need more and more things or be sadly disappointed or hurt when our friends let us down.

The only one who can fill that empty spot in any of us is God. So how do we create a faith in a God we can't see?

First, what is faith? Faith is the belief in our hopes and dreams and helps us believe in the things we can't see. In fact the Bible says in Hebrews chapter 11 verse 1, (or it can look like this Hebrews 11:1) "Faith makes us sure of what we hope for and certain of what we do not see."

In Romans 1:19 and 20 the CEV (*Contemporary English Version*) Bible says, "They know everything that can be known about God, because God has shown it all to them. God's eternal power and character cannot be seen. But from the beginning of creation, God has shown what these are like by all He has made."

So we all have faith. We choose what to have faith in. Whatever our faith is in, our hopes and dreams, we make that faith stronger by reading and studying about those hopes and dreams. The same is true with our faith in God. We need to study more about Him. That's how He becomes real to us. The Bible says in Romans 10:17, "Faith comes by hearing the word of God." Also in II Timothy 3:16 CEV it says, "Everything in the scriptures is God's Word. All of it is useful for teaching and helping people and for correcting them and showing them how to live. The Scriptures train God's servants to do all kinds of good deeds."

Here is a web site you can go to that proves God exists and that the Bible is true by using science. The man who started this study was an atheist (not a believer in God) and through trying to prove God doesn't exist and the Bible isn't His Word, the man became a Christian! https://www.doesgodexist.org

You can also download a Bible app called *youversion*. There are easy to understand versions of the Bible. My favorites are the *Contemporary English Version* and the *New International Version* which was written right from the original ancient manuscripts.

As you read *God has our Backs,* I have written out the scriptures I use, however, you can use your phone app to read the scriptures for yourselves. There are two sections to the Bible: The Old Testament and the New Testament. We now live under the time of the New Testament. I will only highlight a few of the stories and people in the Bible so it will be easier to understand it as the one big story it was written to be.

Knowledge Check

1. If we choose to have faith in God, how can we make our faith stronger?

2. What book can we read that actually has God's words in it so we can learn more about Him?

"Can anything separate us from the love of Christ? Can trouble, suffering, and hard times, or hunger and nakedness, or danger and death?....In everything we have won more than a victory because of Christ who loves us. I am sure that nothing can separate us from God's love—not life or death, not angels or spirits, not the present or the future, and not powers above or powers below. Nothing in all creation can separate us from God's love for us in Christ Jesus our Lord" Romans 8:35, 37-39 CEV

By Amelia

Chapter 2

Close your eyes for a moment and imagine the earth not being here. No animals, plants, water, land or people.

This is where our story begins. In Genesis 1:1 the Bible says, "In the beginning God created the heavens and the earth." So we know that God was in the beginning. It continues to say, "and the Spirit of God was hovering over the waters." So the Holy Spirit was also there. Then in the book of John 1:1 and 3 the Bible says, "In the beginning was the Word, and the Word was with God, and the Word was God. He was with God in the beginning. Through Him all things were made." Then in the same chapter verse 14 says, "The Word became flesh and made His dwelling among us. We have seen His glory, the glory of the one and only, who came from the Father, full of grace and truth." This verse says that the Word that was with God in the beginning, came to earth and lived with us. That was Jesus. Did you notice that <u>Word</u> was capitalized in this verse? Anytime you see <u>Word</u> capitalized you will know that it is talking about Jesus. There are many verses in the Bible that talk about angels being in Heaven but here is an example. In Matthew 18:10 and 11 the CEV Bible says, "Don't be cruel to any of these little ones! (children) I promise you that their angels are always with my Father in Heaven." So in the beginning, God, His Spirit, Jesus, and the angels all lived in Heaven.

Before God made the earth and everything in it, He knew He wanted to make people. He also knew that people would sin in their lives. With sin, we would not be able to go to Heaven and live with God when we die. Romans 6:23 says, "For the wages of sin is death, but the gift of God is eternal life in Christ Jesus our Lord." Before God even made us, He made the big plan to send His son Jesus to the world to save us from our sins so when we die we can live with him forever in Heaven! In I Peter 1:20 and 21 the Bible says Jesus was chosen before the beginning of time. "He was chosen before the creation of the world, but was revealed in these last times for your sake." Also in Ephesians 1:3-5 it says, "Praise be to the God and Father of our Lord Jesus Christ, who has blessed us in the heavenly realms with every spiritual blessing in Christ. For He chose us in Him before the creation of the world to be holy and blameless in His sight."

The first two chapters of Genesis tell exactly how God created everything. In Genesis 1:3 and 8 God made the light and the sky, the first day. In 1:10 God made the land, the second day. In 1:12 God made the plants, the third day. In 1:16 God made the sun, moon and stars, the fourth day. In 1:20 God made the fish and birds, the fifth day. In 1:27 God made the first man and woman, the sixth day.

The first man and woman were named Adam and Eve. Genesis chapter 2 tells how God made them. Genesis 2:7 says, "The Lord God formed the man from the dust of the ground and breathed into his nostrils the breath of life, and the man became a living being." In 2:20 it says, "So the man gave names to all the livestock, the birds of the air and all the beasts of the field. But for Adam no suitable helper was found. So the Lord God caused the man to fall into a deep sleep; and while he was sleeping, he took one of the man's ribs and closed up the place with flesh. Then the Lord God made a woman from the rib He had taken out of the man, and He brought her to the man." Genesis 3:20 says, "Adam named his wife Eve, because she would become the mother of all the living."

Genesis 2:15-17 says, "The Lord God took the man and put him in the Garden of Eden to work it and take care of it. And the Lord God commanded the man, "You are free to eat from any tree in the garden; but you must not eat from the tree of the knowledge of good and evil, for when you eat of it you will surely die."

This is where the devil enters the picture. He came disguised as a serpent and told Eve in Genesis 3:4-5, "you will not surely die, for God knows, when you eat of it your eyes will be opened, and you will be like God knowing good and evil." So Eve ate the fruit and gave some to Adam and that was the first sin in the world. Genesis 3:7 says, "Right away they knew they were naked and they sewed fig leaves together to cover themselves."

God punished Adam, Eve and the serpent. To the serpent in Genesis 3:14 God said, "You will crawl on your stomach and eat dirt all the days of your life." I wonder if this is what the serpent may have looked like then?

The way Jesus crushed Satan's head was by being hung on the cross and paying for our sins. Jesus also rose from the dead proving Satan had no power to keep Jesus dead and in the grave. Hebrews 2:14 CEV says, "We are people of flesh and blood. That is why Jesus became one of us. He died to destroy the devil, who had power over death. But He also died to rescue all of us who live each day in fear of dying." So part of Satan's punishment was that Jesus would take away his power to spiritually keep us dead and separated from God by our sins forever.

The way Satan struck Jesus' heel was when Jesus was physically hung on the cross. That physically hurt Jesus' body.

God continues in verse 5 saying, "And I will put enmity (hatred) between you and the woman, and between your seed and hers." This actually was the first promise of Jesus. This seed of woman is talking about Jesus. Man's seed was not involved because Jesus' mother was a virgin. God continues to say, "He (Jesus) will crush your (Satan's) head, and you (Satan) will strike His (Jesus') heel."

To Eve God said in Genesis 3:16, "You will suffer terribly when you give birth, you will desire your husband and he will rule over you." To Adam God said in Genesis 3:17-19, "You listened to your wife and ate fruit from that tree. And so, the ground will be under a curse because of what you did. As long as you live, you will have to struggle to grow enough food. Your food will be plants, but the ground will produce thorns and thistles. You will have to sweat to earn a living: you were made out of soil, and you will once again turn into soil.

God knew all this would happen and now starts God's big plan to bring Jesus to earth to save us.

Adam and Eve had children and in God's plan Jesus was going to be born from one of those children. Jesus was coming from their son named Seth. We can read in the Bible the list of Jesus' ancestors in Matthew chapter 1 and Luke chapter 3. Luke 3:38 says at the end of the verse, "Seth, the son of Adam, the son of God."

God's Plan For Jesus

Saving Jesus' Ancestors

Adam

Seth

Knowledge Check

1. After God made everything, who was the first man and woman He made?

2. Where did Adam and Eve live?

3. The devil talked Eve into sinning. What was the first sin?

4. Who did God plan to send to save us from our sins?

5. Which son of Adam and Eve was Jesus coming from?

By Izzy

10

Chapter 3

All the stories in the Old Testament in the Bible are about the people in Jesus' ancestry. They are about how God made sure all of Jesus' ancestors were kept safe so Jesus would eventually be born on earth to save us from our sins.

In Genesis 6:1 the CEV Bible says, "More and more people were born until finally they spread all over the earth." Now sin had been on the earth for quite awhile and Genesis 6:5-22 says, "The Lord saw how bad the people on the earth were and that everything they thought and planned was evil. He was sorry that He had made them, and He said, "I'll destroy every living creature on earth!....I'm sorry I ever made them.... But the Lord was pleased with a man named Noah and this is the story about him. Noah obeyed God. He had three sons, Shem, Ham and Japheth. God told Noah to build an Ark. Make rooms in it and cover it with tar inside and out. Make it 450 feet long, 75 feet wide and 45 feet high. Build a roof on the boat and leave a space of 18" between the roof and the sides. Make it 3 stories high and put a door on one side. I'm going to send a flood that will destroy everything that breathes. But I promise you, your wife, your sons, and their wives will be kept safe in the Ark. Bring into the ark with you a male and female of every kind of animal, bird and reptile. I don't want them destroyed. Store up enough food for yourself and them." Then Genesis 7:2-3 in the CEV Bible God told Noah, "Take 7 pairs of every kind of animal that can be used for sacrifices and one pair of all the others. Also take seven pairs of every kind of bird with you, so there will always be animals and birds on the earth. Noah did everything the Lord told him to do."

The rest of the story is in Genesis 7:17-8:22. Then it rained for 40 days and nights. Nothing was left living on the earth except Noah and the others on the Ark. One Hundred and fifty days later, God made a wind blow and the water started going down. Soon Noah and all who were on the ark came out on dry land. Noah built an altar to the Lord and sacrificed one of each of the animals that could be used for a sacrifice to God.

Genesis 9:12-17 says God was pleased with Noah and made him and all of us a promise. He promised to never again destroy everything on the earth with a flood. Then God put a rainbow in the sky as a sign of His promise.

God told Noah and his family to have many children and fill the earth with people again. Remember God's plan to bring Jesus to the earth? God saved Noah and his family from the flood because Jesus was coming from Noah's son Shem. You can find Shem's name in Jesus' ancestry in Luke 3:36.

God's Plan For Jesus

Saving Jesus' Ancestors

Adam

⬇

Seth

⬇

Noah

⬇

Shem

Knowledge Check

1. Whose ancestors was God protecting throughout the Old Testament of the Bible?

2. Why did God want to destroy everyone on earth?

3. Whose family loved God and was kept safe during the flood?

4. Which of Noah's sons was Jesus coming from?

By Lily

14

Chapter 4

Noah's family did as God told them and had children and grandchildren. Soon a man named Abraham was born as one of Shem's great grandchildren. In Genesis 12:2-7 God makes **3 Promises** to Abraham. I will list them in the order they come true in the Bible.

The **First Promise** in Genesis 12:2 is, "I will make you into a great nation." Then in Genesis 15:5 God told Abraham to "look up into the heavens and count the stars—if indeed you can count them. Then he said to him, "so shall your offspring be."

The **Second Promise** in Genesis 12:7 is, "To your offspring, I will give the land of Canaan." In Genesis 17:8 God says, "The whole land of Canaan, where you are now an alien, I will give as an everlasting possession to you and your descendants after you; and I will be their God."

The **Third Promise** in Genesis 12:3 is, …. "and all people on earth will be blessed through you." In the New Testament, Galatians 3:8 and 14 says, "God announced the gospel in advance to Abraham, all nations will be blessed through you." and in verse 14 it says, "He redeemed us in order that the blessing given to Abraham might come to the Gentiles through Jesus Christ." Then in Galatians 3:29 the Bible says, "So if you belong to Christ, you are now part of Abraham's family and heirs according to the promise." Jesus was going to be the blessing for all people. Jesus was coming from Abraham in Luke 3:34.

Saving Jesus' Ancestors

God's Plan For Jesus

Adam

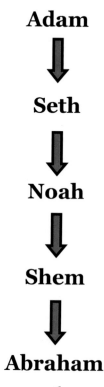

Seth

Noah

Shem

Abraham

16

Knowledge Check

1. Who was Shem's great, great grandchild?

2. What were the three promises God made to Abraham?

3. Who was Jesus coming from in this story?

By Colette

18

Chapter 5

In this chapter we will begin with the **First Promise** God made to Abraham. Genesis 12:2 says, "I will make you into a great nation" (huge family). It all started with Abraham and his wife Sarah. Their story of the huge family starts in Genesis 18:15 through Genesis 30:24.

When Abraham and Sarah were very old, God promised they would have a son and his name would be Isaac. Sarah and Abraham both laughed about this promise because Abraham was 100 years old and Sarah was 90. But it came true and in Genesis 21:1-3 the Bible says, "Now the Lord was   gracious to Sarah as He had said, and the Lord did for Sarah what He had promised." Sarah became pregnant and bore a son...Abraham gave the name Isaac to the son.

When Isaac was 40 years old he married a woman named Rebekah and she had twins, Jacob and Esau. In Luke 3:34 it says Jesus was going to come from Jacob. After Jacob grew to be a man he was a great start to the huge family God promised. He had 12 sons! Their names were Issachar, Zebulun, Judah, Reuben, Simeon, Levi, Benjamin, Dan, Naphtali, Gad, Asher, and Joseph. Which of the twelve sons do you think Jesus was coming from? In Luke 3:33 Judah is the one listed in Jesus' ancestry.

God's Plan For Jesus
Saving Jesus' Ancestors

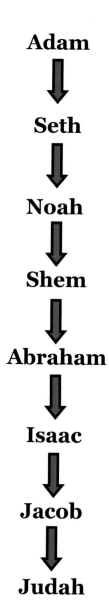

Adam

Seth

Noah

Shem

Abraham

Isaac

Jacob

Judah

Knowledge Check

1. Who was the son God promised to Abraham and Sarah?

2. When Isaac married what were his twin son's names?

3. Which twin son was Jesus coming from?

4. To start the huge family promise, how many children did Jacob have?

5. Which one of the 12 children was Jesus coming from?

By Isaac

Chapter 6

This part of our story is found in Genesis chapter 37 and is about one of Jacob's sons named Joseph. Jacob loved Joseph very much and gave him a special beautiful coat of many colors. Joseph's brothers were very jealous of Joseph.

One day Jacob asked Joseph to go find his brothers who were watching their sheep in a field. Joseph left and in his searching finally found them. When Joseph's brothers saw him coming, they quickly made a plan to get rid of Joseph. Poor Joseph had no idea what they were planning. When Joseph got close enough, his brothers grabbed him and threw him into an old dried up well.

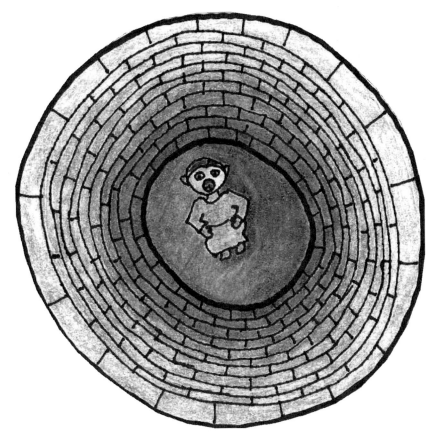

Later on, the same day, the brothers were eating their lunch. All of a sudden they saw some men coming down the road nearby. The brothers quickly came up with a new plan to get rid of Joseph. When the men were close enough, the brothers stopped them and asked where they were going. The men said they were on their way to a country called Egypt. That sounded perfect to the brothers. They made a deal with the men and sold Joseph to them. The men would take Joseph with them to Egypt and the brothers would be rid of him forever.

God is going to use Joseph after he goes to live in Egypt. The brothers did not know it but this was all part of God's plan to bring Jesus from Joseph's brother Judah. Judah is listed in Jesus' ancestry in Luke 3:33.

God's Plan For Jesus
Saving Jesus' Ancestors

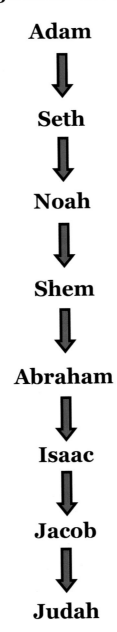

Adam

Seth

Noah

Shem

Abraham

Isaac

Jacob

Judah

Knowledge Check

1. Why was Joseph's brothers jealous of him?

2. What was the first thing the brothers did to get rid of Joseph?

3. What was the second thing they did to Joseph?

4. Was Joseph used in God's plan to bring Jesus?

5. Which brother was Jesus coming from?

By Ethan

Chapter 7

This part of our story is from Genesis chapters 39-47. It starts after Joseph was taken to Egypt and had been there a few years. The most important man in Egypt called Pharaoh had gone to bed one night and had a strange dream. It was about cows and grain. It was so strange that Pharaoh wanted to know what it meant. That day many men tried to interpret Pharaoh's dream and failed. Joseph heard about this and knew he could interpret his dream with God's help. So he went to Pharaoh and was able to tell him what his dream meant.

Joseph said all the land and the people were going to have seven years of plenty of food growing in the fields. Then the next seven years there would be a famine when no food would grow at all.

Pharaoh was so happy to know what his dream meant that he put Joseph in charge of all the land and food. Pharaoh told Joseph that during the first seven years when they had plenty of food, Joseph should save some of the food every year. Then when the next seven years of famine came, Joseph could pass out the food to the hungry people. Pharaoh knew he could trust Joseph and grew to love him very much.

Everything happened just as Joseph told Pharaoh it would. The first seven years there was plenty and Joseph saved part of the food every year. When the next seven years came, Joseph gave food to the hungry people.

It wasn't long before Joseph's own brothers came to him for food. Joseph knew who they were, but his brothers didn't recognize him. By this time Joseph was a man and was no longer the boy they threw into the well.

Joseph was so happy to see his brothers he cried and later told them who he was. He said, "Remember me? Your brother Joseph you threw into the well?" His brothers were very scared. But Joseph told them not to be afraid because it was God's plan to send him to Egypt.

When Pharaoh found out Joseph's family came for food, Pharaoh wanted them all to come live in Egypt. He gave them the best land and everything they needed. The brothers went back home and got their father, Jacob. They took him to the new land in Egypt. Joseph went to see his father that he had not seen in such a long time. When they saw each other they cried and cried they were so happy!

Joseph's family was saved from starving and they had many, many children while they lived in Egypt. This family became the huge family God promised to Abraham in Genesis 12:2. They were called the Israelites. God's **First Promise** came true! In Genesis 47:27 the Bible says, "Now the Israelites settled in Egypt in the region of Goshen. They acquired property there and were fruitful and increased greatly in number." God told Abraham, "I will make your family huge, as many as the stars!" It happened just as God promised.

God's plan is moving right along as Jesus will be coming from Judah, one of the Israelites. Judah is listed in Jesus ancestry in Luke 3:33.

God's Plan For Jesus
Saving Jesus' Ancestors

Adam

Seth

Noah

Shem

Abraham

Isaac

Jacob

Judah

Knowledge Check

1. Who told Pharaoh what his dream meant?

2. What did his dream mean?

3. After Joseph was put in charge, who came asking for food?

4. Pharaoh told Joseph's family to stay in Egypt and while they were there which Promise came true?

By Jade

Chapter 8

After the Israelites became the huge family God promised Abraham, a new Pharaoh became the leader in Egypt. This story is found in Exodus chapters 1 and 2.

The new Pharaoh did not know about Joseph or how he saved the people from starving. He also didn't know how much the other Pharaoh loved Joseph and his huge family. This Pharaoh only knew there were so many Israelites, he was afraid they would take over his land!

The new Pharaoh decided to make the Israelites work very hard and do all the work for the people who lived in Egypt first, called Egyptians. God's huge family, the Israelites, also were not allowed to worship God anymore. How horrible that must have been! But this mean Pharaoh could not stop God's plan to bring Jesus from the Israelite Judah.

As time went on, the Israelites kept growing and became an even bigger family of people. This scared Pharaoh even more! So he made a new rule. All the boy babies the Israelites had would be thrown into the river to die. The midwives, however, feared God and did not do what the new rule said and they let the baby boys live.

One of the boy baby's name was Moses. Moses' mom made a basket for him and put him inside. Then she floated the basket safely in the river to hide Moses from Pharaoh. Moses' sister Miriam watched over him as he floated, making sure he was safe.

Moses floated for awhile and soon a woman spotted him. But she wasn't just any woman, she was Pharaoh's own daughter. Miriam thought quickly and offered to get a woman to be a babysitter for Pharaoh's daughter. The daughter agreed and Miriam ran and brought their own Mom to take care of Moses. Do you think that was a coincidence? God sure is at work!

As Moses grew, he continued to live with Pharaoh's daughter. But with his own Mom taking care of him, he knew he was really an Israelite and not an Egyptian. God is going to use Moses in His plan to bring Jesus from the Israelite Judah. Once again Luke 3:33 lists Judah in Jesus' ancestry.

God's Plan For Jesus
Saving Jesus' Ancestors

Adam	Abraham
⬇	⬇
Seth	Isaac
⬇	⬇
Noah	Jacob
⬇	⬇
Shem	Judah

Knowledge Check

1. When Egypt had a new Pharaoh, why didn't he like the Israelites?

2. What horrible thing did Pharaoh do to try and stop the Israelites family from getting bigger?

3. Who did God save in this story to use in His plan to bring Jesus?

4. Who is Jesus coming from in the Israelites?

By Jade

34

Chapter 9

This part of our story starts in Exodus chapters 4-12. Moses is now a full grown man. God saw how badly the Egyptians were treating His people, the Israelites. God didn't like it at all. He wanted Pharaoh to let His people go! God talked to Moses and said, "Moses, go tell Pharaoh to let my people go!" Moses really didn't want to do this because he had a hard time talking. So God sent Moses' brother Aaron with him. Moses and Aaron told Pharaoh that God said to let His people go! Pharaoh looked at Moses and just said, "No!"

God knew what Pharaoh said and decided to change Pharaoh's mind. The first thing God did was change all their water in Egypt to blood. But when Moses and Aaron went to Pharaoh again and asked to let the Israelites go, Pharaoh still said, "No!"

God continued to change Pharaoh's mind. Next God sent frogs, gnats, and flies to bother Pharaoh and the Egyptians. They were everywhere, their houses, beds, and food. Everywhere they walked they would get squished under their feet. But even that did not work! When Moses and Aaron asked again, Pharaoh still said, "No!"

This time God made some of their animals die and made sores all over Pharaoh and the Egyptian's bodies. But when Moses and Aaron asked to let the Israelites go, Pharaoh still said, "No!"

Next God made it hail everywhere in Egypt! The whole ground was covered. They wouldn't be able to walk outside without getting hit with hail. But once again Pharaoh still said, "No!"

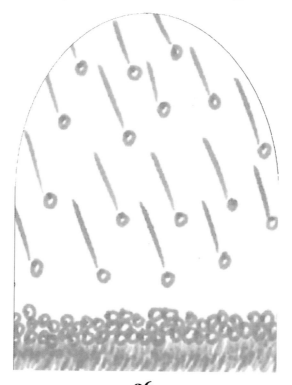

After God sent the hail He sent grasshoppers! Millions of grasshoppers! Can you just picture them hopping everywhere? They were in their houses, food, and squished under their feet! But Pharaoh still said, "No!"

Finally God did one more thing to change Pharaoh's mind. This time God killed the oldest child in each of the Egyptian families including Pharaoh's. Then God killed the oldest in the animal families as well. That would have been the worst thing God did so far. This time Pharaoh called Moses and Aaron to him and said, "Take the Israelites, their animals, all of their belongings and leave!" Finally! They were finally going to be free! Remember God is using Moses to save the Israelites because Jesus is coming from Judah in Luke 3:33.

God's Plan For Jesus
Saving Jesus' Ancestors

Adam

Seth

Noah

Shem

Abraham

Isaac

Jacob

Judah

Knowledge Check

1. What did God tell Moses and Aron to ask Pharaoh?

2. What were some of the things God did to make Pharaoh want to let God's people go?

3. Did Pharaoh ever let God's people go?

4. Who was Jesus coming from in the Israelites?

By Connor

40

Chapter 10

After Pharaoh finally let the Israelites go, our story will span over Exodus 12 through Joshua 24. In fact you can read a summary of this story in Joshua chapter 24.

Now Moses wasted no time and gathered the Israelites, their belongings, and animals and left that horrible country of Egypt. The Israelites were very happy on their journey. They even sang and danced along the way.

The Israelites walked and walked until they came to a big body of water called the Red Sea. They all stopped and wondered how they would get across the great expanse of water. All of a sudden they heard something! They turned around and saw Pharaoh's whole army coming after them! The Israelites didn't know it but after they left, Pharaoh had changed his mind and sent his army to bring the Israelites back to Egypt. The Israelites were very afraid, but they shouldn't have been because they were God's people. God took care of them all this time because Jesus was coming from them. Just then God told Moses to hold his rod over the water! Moses did as he was told. The water opened up all the way and they walked across on dry ground. That was amazing!

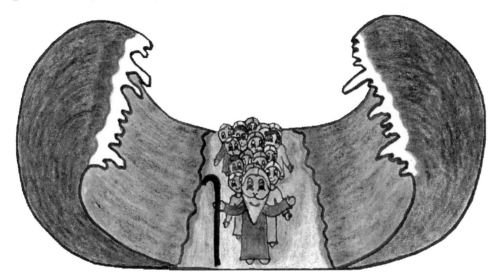

When everyone and all the animals were across, Moses looked back and saw Pharaoh's whole army coming across too! God then told Moses to stretch his hand back out over the water. Moses again did as he was told and God made the water fall on the whole Egyptian army and they were all drowned!

The Israelites continued on their journey and headed for the land of Canaan. This was the land God had promised to them in the **Second Promise** to Abraham. The Israelites traveled 40 years and God saved them from trouble many, many times.

It took a long time to travel to Canaan. When they got fairly close, God showed Moses the land and after that Moses died. God then had a man named Joshua lead the Israelites. He was a good man and God Helped him lead the people just like He helped Moses.

The day finally came and the Israelites walked into the land of Canaan. God's **Second Promise** to Abraham came true! In Genesis 12:7 God told Abraham, "To your huge family I will give the land of Canaan! Then in Joshua 21:43 it says, "So the Lord gave the Israelites the land He had promised their ancestors and they took possession of it and settled there."

God did all of this to show the Israelites that He would always go before them and fight their battles. Also that they did not get to the promised land of Canaan on their own. Just like we will not get to Heaven on our own or by just being good. Remember God's big plan to bring Jesus? Jesus is coming from the Israelite Judah listed in Luke 3:33

God's Plan For Jesus

Saving Jesus' Ancestors

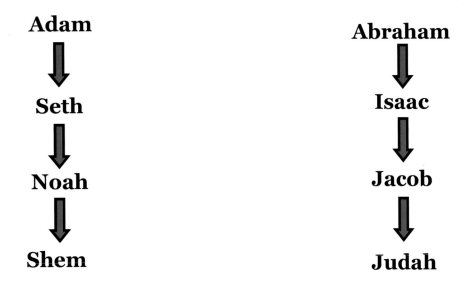

Knowledge Check

1. When the Israelites left Egypt, what did God do when they came to the Red Sea?

2. When Pharaoh's army came after them and tried to cross the Red Sea, what did God do?

3. After the Israelites' long travels what land did God give them?

4. What Promise came true in this story?

5. Which Israelite was Jesus coming from?

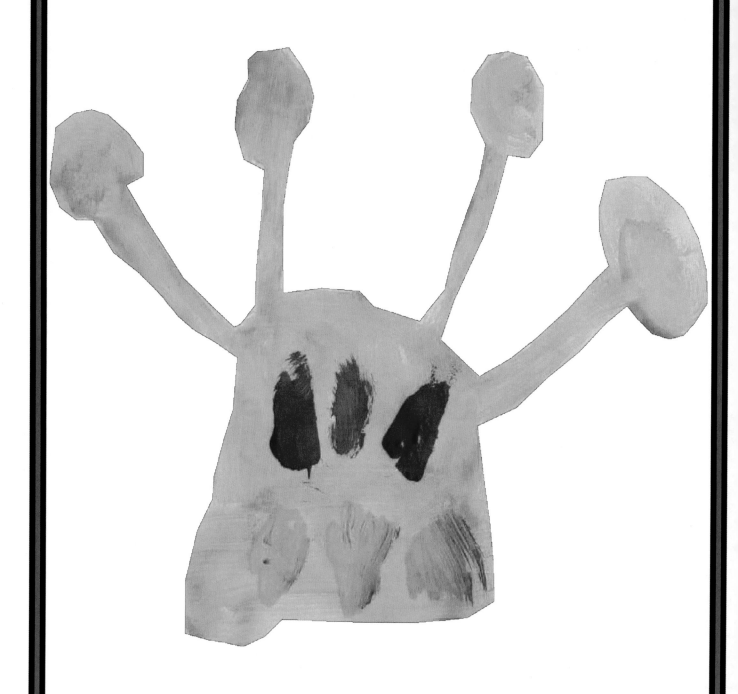

"The Crown" by Connor

Chapter 11

This story comes from I Samuel chapter 8 to I Kings chapter 2. After the Israelites were settled in their new land, they were happy for awhile. Then they began to notice all the countries around them had Kings. They had forgotten God was the greatest King they could ever have! Soon they started pestering God about giving them a King. Finally God told them He would give them one.

Some of the Kings the Israelites had, loved God and some Kings did not. There was one King who was a very special King. His name was King David. King David loved God very much and took good care of God's people. He also loved to play his harp and sing for God and God loved listening to him play.

After David had been King for a time, he decided he wanted a wife. He chose to marry a beautiful woman name Bathsheba.

Through their life together, King David and Bathsheba had children. Two of their children were named Solomon and Nathan. These two were going to be ancestors of Jesus' mother and earthly father. So Jesus was coming from King David and Bathsheba.

God's Plan For Jesus
Saving Jesus' Ancestors

Adam	**Isaac**
⬇	⬇
Seth	**Jacob**
⬇	⬇
Noah	**Judah**
⬇	⬇
Shem	**David and Bathsheba**
⬇	
Abraham	

The rest of the Old Testament contains books about everything that happened to the Israelites between the time of King David and when Christ comes in the beginning of the New Testament. There are books of rules for the Israelites to follow and books about the different Kings and Judges they had ruling over them. Also there are books written by people called prophets. The prophets foretold about Jesus coming so the Israelites did not get discouraged. They had to wait many years for Jesus to come to earth to save us from our sins.

Knowledge Check

1. After the Israelites were living in Canaan, what did they pester God about giving them?

2. What was one of their good King's name?

3. Who did he marry?

4. Who was Jesus mother, Mary, and earthly father, Joseph, coming from?

Afghan by Amelia

Chapter 12

In God's plan so far, He is sending Jesus to save us and Jesus was coming from Seth! When the whole world was wicked, God saved Noah because Jesus was coming from Shem! Next God made **3 Promises** to Abraham. **1.** The huge family **2.** The land of Canaan. **3.** The blessing through Abraham. Jesus was the blessing. The **First Promise** started to come true with Abraham, Isaac, Jacob, and 12 sons. Jesus was coming from the son named Judah. One of the 12 sons named Joseph ended up in Egypt as part of God's plan. He saved his own family from starving. Joseph's family moved to Egypt and the **First Promise** came true. They became the huge family God promised to Abraham that Jesus was coming from. Soon there was a new Pharaoh who did not like how big the Israelite family had grown. He wanted to kill all the boy babies but the midwives did not follow the new law. A baby named Moses was saved and raised by Pharaoh's daughter with his mom as a baby sitter. After Moses grew into a man and led the Israelites out of Egypt, God finally gave them the land of Canaan. The **Second Promise** came true! Jesus was coming from Judah! After the Israelites settled in Canaan they wanted a king. God gave them kings. Some were bad, others were good. King David was one who loved God very much. He chose a wife Bathsheba and Jesus was coming from their two sons Nathan and Solomon. They are listed in I Chronicles 3:5 as being sons of King David and Bathsheba.

In Luke 3:31 Nathan is listed in Jesus' ancestry as the son of David. In this list Mary, Jesus' mother, came from Nathan, as Mary's father, Heli, is listed in Luke 3:23. It was a custom then to list the head of the household in the ancestry list instead of the women.

Then in Matthew 1:7 Solomon is listed instead of Nathan as being David's son. In this list of Jesus' ancestry Joseph, Jesus' earthly father, is listed in Matthew 1:16 as being Mary's husband. Mary and Joseph were both listed as coming from David and Bathsheba. Which means Jesus came from them as well.

David   Bathsheba

Nathan

Solomon

Mary

Joseph

Now we know who Mary and Joseph were and who they came from. We also know God's plan for Jesus can be traced through the entire Bible. In this chapter of our story Jesus is finally here!!! This story is found in Luke 1:26-38 and 2:1-20.

Starting in Luke 1:26 the CEV Bible says, ".......God sent the angel Gabriel to the town of Nazareth in Galilee with a message for a virgin named Mary. She was engaged to Joseph from the family of King David. The angel greeted Mary and said, "You are truly blessed! The Lord is with you." Mary was confused by the angel's words and wondered what they meant. The angel told Mary, Don't be afraid! God is pleased with you, and you will have a son. His name will be Jesus. He will be great and will be called the Son of God Most High. The Lord God will make Him King, as His ancestor David was. He will rule the people of Israel forever, and His kingdom will never end."

Mary asked the angel, "How can this happen? I am not married!" The Angel answered, "The Holy Spirit will come down to you, and God's power will come over you. So your child will be called the Holy Son of God. Your relative Elizabeth is also going to have a son, even though she is old. No one thought she could ever have a baby, but in three months she will have a son. Nothing is impossible for God!" Mary said, "I am the Lord's servant! Let it happen as you have said." And the angel left her."

"About that time Emperor Augustus gave orders for the names of all the people to be listed in record books. These first records were made when Quirinius was governor of Syria. Everyone had to go to their own hometown to be listed. So Joseph had to leave Nazareth in Galilee and go to Bethlehem in Judea. Long ago Bethlehem had been King David's hometown, and Joseph went there because he was from David's family. Mary was engaged to Joseph and traveled with him to Bethlehem. She was soon going to have a baby, and while they were there, she gave birth to her first-born son. She dressed Him in baby clothes and laid Him on a bed of hay, because there was no room for them in the inn."

"That night in the fields near Bethlehem some shepherds were guarding their sheep. All at once an angel came down to them from the Lord, and the brightness of the Lord's glory flashed around them! The shepherds were frightened! But the angel said, "Don't be afraid! I have good news for you, which will make everyone happy. This very day in King David's hometown a Savior was born for you. He is Christ the Lord. You will know who He is, because you will find Him dressed in baby clothes and lying on a bed of hay.""

Suddenly many other angels came down from Heaven and joined in praising God. They said: "Praise God in Heaven! Peace on earth, goodwill to men!" After the angels had left and gone back to Heaven, the shepherds said to each other. "Let's go to Bethlehem and see what the Lord has told us about."

"They hurried off and found Mary and Joseph, and they saw the baby lying in a manger. When the shepherds saw Jesus, they told His parents what the angel had said about Him. Everyone listened and was surprised. But Mary kept thinking about all this and wondering what it meant."

The **Third Promise** to Abraham in Genesis 12:3 "all people will be blessed through you" has come true! Galatians 3:8 says.... "God told Abraham the good news that all nations would be blessed through you. So those who have faith are blessed along with Abraham, the man of faith."

God's Plan For Jesus
Saving Jesus' Ancestors

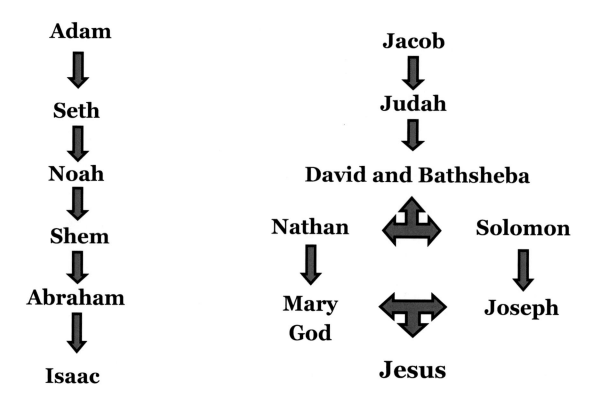

Knowledge Check

1. What plan can be traced through the entire Bible?

2. Who came to tell Mary she was going to have baby Jesus?

3. What town was Jesus born in?

4. Who told the shepherds about Jesus being born?

5. Which promise is coming true because Jesus is born?

By Noah

Chapter 13

Jesus didn't stay a baby long. He grew and grew and soon became a full grown man. When Jesus was about 30 years old, He knew there was a man named John the Baptist baptizing people in the Jordon River. In Matthew 3:13-17 the CEV Bible says, "Jesus left Galilee and went to the Jordan River to be baptized by John. But John kept objecting and said, "I ought to be baptized by you. Why have you come to me?" Jesus answered, "For now this is how it should be, because we must do all that God wants us to do." Then John agreed. So Jesus was baptized.

As soon as He came out of the water the sky opened, and he saw the Spirit of God coming down on Him like a dove. And a voice from heaven said, "This is my Son, whom I love; with Him I am well pleased."

After Jesus was baptized the CEV Bible says in Matthew 4:23-25, "Jesus went all over Galilee, teaching in the Jewish meeting places and preaching the good news about God's kingdom. He also healed every kind of disease and sickness. Many people followed Jesus. In Matthew chapters 5, 6 and 7, Jesus preached to them from a mountainside. In chapter 5 He listed attitudes we should live by. He said to be meek, merciful, pure in heart and peacemakers. He also said not to loose control of our tempers, love your enemies and pray for those who are mean to you. Then in chapters 6 and 7, Jesus said to give to the needy, always pray, not to worry, and not to judge others. He goes on to say, that everyone who hears these words and puts them into practice is like a wise man who built his house on a rock. The rain and wind came and couldn't blow his house down. These are all attitudes and instructions on living a Godly life while we are here on earth. In Matthew 7:28 it says, "When Jesus had finished speaking, the crowds were amazed at His teaching because He taught as one who had authority..." More and more people heard that Jesus was finally here! The one who came to save   everyone from their sins! They were so excited because they had waited so long for Him!

As Jesus went all around the land teaching and healing, He also chose men to spread the news and help Him heal the people. In Matthew 4:18-19 the CEV Bible says, "Jesus was walking along the shore of Lake Galilee and saw two brothers fishing, casting their nets from a boat.... "Jesus said to them, "Come with me! I will teach you how to bring in people instead of fish." Right then the two brothers dropped their nets and went with Him." This kind of thing happened until Jesus had twelve good men to help Him.

Then in Matthew 10:1-4 "Jesus gathered the twelve men together and gave them the power to drive out evil spirits and to heal every kind of disease and sickness." These men were called Apostles. Their names are listed as, "Peter, Andrew, James, John, Philip, Bartholomew, Thomas, Matthew, James son of Alphaeus, Thaddaeus, Simon, and Judas Iscariot."

In Matthew 10:7-42, in the CEV Bible, Jesus gave the Apostles instructions before He sent them out to teach. Jesus said, "Announce that the Kingdom will soon be here, heal the sick, raise the dead to life,...don't take along any gold,...traveling bag or an extra shirt or sandals..... Don't be afraid of people. They can kill you, but not your soul. Instead you should fear God who can destroy both your body and soul in hell.... Aren't two sparrows sold for only a penny? (Cheap) But your Father (in Heaven) knows when any one of them falls to the ground. Even the hairs on your head are counted. So don't be afraid! You are worth much more than many sparrows."

The rest of Matthew, Mark, Luke and John is the continued life story of Jesus, while He was on the earth.

Knowledge Check

1. When Jesus was a man, who baptized Him?

2. What did God say when He came up out of the water?

3. After Jesus was baptized what did He go around doing?

4. How many men did Jesus choose to help Him teach the people?

5. When Jesus sent the apostles to teach, what were some of the instructions He gave them?

By Lily

60

Chapter 14

Throughout Jesus' life, some of the people loved Jesus and believed everything He taught them. But some of the people didn't believe Jesus was God's son. They were angry because Jesus kept telling them this. Some people grew so angry they wanted to kill Jesus.

One of Jesus own Apostles named Judas betrayed Jesus for 30 pieces of silver. In Matthew 26:47-50 the CEV Bible says, "Judas came to Jesus with a large mob of men armed with swords and clubs. Judas told the mob ahead of time; "arrest the man I greet with a kiss." Judas kissed Jesus and Jesus said, "My friend, do what you came for." The men grabbed Jesus and arrested Him. In verse 56 Jesus says, "But all this happened, so that what the prophets wrote would come true." This was all part of God's big plan for Jesus.

In Matthew 27:1-60 the CEV Bible says, Jesus went to trial and the people kept yelling, "crucify Him, crucify Him". "The soldiers were ordered to beat Jesus with a whip and nail Him to a cross... They stuck a crown of thorns on His head....They came to a place named Golgotha, which means "Place of a Skull."

"..The soldiers nailed Jesus to the cross...At noon the sky turned dark and stayed that way till 3 o'clock. Then Jesus said, "My God, My God why have you deserted Me?" ...Then when Jesus cried out again in a loud voice, He gave up His spirit... At that moment the earth shook and rocks split....When the centurion and those with him who were guarding Jesus saw the earthquake and all that had happened, they were terrified and exclaimed, "Surely He was the Son of God!"... "Then a man named Joseph from the town Arimathea took Jesus' body and wrapped it in a clean linen cloth. He put Jesus' body in a tomb cut into solid rock...He rolled a big stone against the entrance and went away..." Jesus took our punishment for our sins on Himself. II Corinthians 5:21 says, "God made Him (Jesus) who had no sin to be sin for us, so that in Him we might become the righteousness of God."

In Matthew 27:64-28:17, the CEV says, "Jesus' Tomb was guarded for 3 days... Mary Magdalene and the other Mary went to see the tomb. Suddenly a strong earthquake struck, and the Lord's angel came down from Heaven. He rolled the stone away and sat on it. The angel looked as bright as lightening and his clothes were as white as snow. The guards shook with fear and fell down as if they were dead. The angel said to the women, "Don't be afraid! I know you are looking for Jesus, who was nailed to a cross. He isn't here! God has raised Him to life just as Jesus said He would. ...Come see the place where His body was lying."

"Now hurry, tell His disciples that He has been raised to life and is on His way to Galilee. Go there and you will see Him. That is what I came to tell you." The women were frightened and very happy and ran to tell His disciples. Suddenly Jesus met them and greeted them. They went near Him... and worshipped Him. Then Jesus said, "Don't be afraid, tell My followers to go to Galilee. They will see Me there..."

"...Jesus' disciples went to a mountain in Galilee...they saw Him and worshipped Him..." In Mark 16:15-20 the CEV Bible says, "Jesus said to them, Go and preach the good news to everyone in the world. Anyone who believes Me and is baptized will be saved. But anyone who refuses to believe Me will be condemned... After the Lord Jesus had said these things to the Apostles, He was taken back up to Heaven where He sat down at the right side of God. Then the Apostles left and preached everywhere. The Lord was with them and the miracles they did proved that their message was true!"

Knowledge Check

1. Some people didn't believe that Jesus was God's son, what did they do to Him?

2. What things happened when Jesus was crucified that made the people realize He was God's son?

3. Who took our punishment for our sin on Himself?

4. What happened after Jesus was in the tomb for three days?

5. According to what Jesus told the apostles, what will happen to anyone who believes and is baptized?

By Noah

66

Chapter 15

In God's plan so far, Jesus was coming from Seth! God saved Noah because Jesus was coming from Shem! Next God made **3 promises** to Abraham. **1.** The huge family **2.** The land of Canaan. **3.** The blessing through Abraham that was Jesus. The **First Promise** began with Abraham, Isaac, Jacob, and 12 sons. Jesus was coming from the son named Judah.

One of the 12 sons named Joseph was taken to Egypt as part of God's plan and saved the huge family Jesus was coming from. Soon there was a new Pharaoh who did not like how big the Israelite family had grown. He wanted to kill all the boy babies. Moses was born and his Mom put him in a basket in the river. Pharaoh's daughter found him and kept him. With Moses' own Mom as his babysitter he grew up to know he was really an Israelite.

Later Moses led the Israelites out of Egypt. God did many things to help them along their way to the promised land of Canaan. After many years, God finally gave them the land which meant the **Second Promise** came true. Remember Jesus was coming from the Israelite, Judah!

After the Israelites settled in Canaan God gave them kings. King David loved God very much. He chose a wife Bathsheba and they had Nathan and Solomon. Mary came from Nathan and Joseph came from Solomon. They grew and were married and they had baby Jesus in a manger. God was Jesus Father in Heaven and Joseph was His dad on earth. Jesus was the **Third Promise** to Abraham that came true! All people would be blessed because Jesus had come to take away our sins!

When Jesus grew to be a man, He was baptized by John the Baptist. God told Jesus He was pleased with Him! After Jesus was baptized He went everywhere teaching the people and doing wonderful things called miracles so they would believe He was God's Son. There were so many people Jesus chose twelve men to help Him teach.

Some of the people were angry when Jesus said He was God's Son; so angry they hung Jesus on a cross. They did not know this was all part of God's plan that Jesus would die on the cross, be buried, and after three days come to life again! God gave His Son to save us from our sins!

After Jesus went back to Heaven, in Acts 2, God sent His Holy Spirit to earth. The Apostles received the Holy Spirit and were able to speak in the languages of the people from different nations who were gathered in Jerusalem. When the Apostles started speaking to the people, they were amazed and perplexed that they could hear the apostles in their own languages. Then in Acts 2:22-47 the CEV Bible says, "Peter stood up and said, "Now listen to what I have to say about Jesus from Nazareth. God proved that He sent Jesus to you by having Him work miracles, wonders and signs. All of you know this. God had already planned and decided that Jesus would be handed over to you. So you took Him and had evil men put Him to death on a cross. But God set Him free from death and raised Him to life. Death could not hold Him in it's power..."

"When the people heard this, they were very upset. They asked Peter and the other Apostles, "Friends, what shall we do?" Peter said, "Turn back to God! Be baptized in the name of Jesus Christ, so that your sins will be forgiven. Then you will be given the Holy Spirit. This promise is for you and your children and for all who are far off- for all who the Lord our God will call." With many other words he warned them, he pleaded with them, "Save yourselves from this corrupt generation......"

"Those who accepted his message were baptized, and about three thousand were added to their number that day...all the believers were together and had everything in common. They sold possessions and gave to anyone that needed it. They ate together in their homes with glad and sincere hearts, praising God and enjoying the favor of all the people. The Lord added to their number daily those who were being saved." They were the first people in Jesus Church!

Being baptized is copying what happened to Jesus. Jesus died and was buried—we die to our old selves and are buried when we go under the water. Then Jesus raised up from the dead and we are raised up out of the water a new forgiven person. In Colossians 2:12 and 13 the CEV Bible says, "...And when you were baptized, it was the same as being buried with Christ. Then you were raised to life because you had faith in the power of God, who raised Christ from death. You were dead, because you were sinful and were not God's people. But God made you alive with Christ. He forgave us all our sins.." Romans 6:4 the CEV Bible says, "...when we were baptized, we died and were buried with Christ. We were baptized, so that we would live a new life, as Christ was raised to life by the glory of the Father." Galatians 3:27 says, "You are all sons of God through faith in Christ Jesus, for all of you who were baptized into Christ have clothed yourselves with Christ. ...if you belong to Christ, then you are Abraham's seed, and heirs according to the **(Third) Promise**." (All people will be blessed through Abraham.)

Knowledge Check

1. What did Peter tell the people they should do after they knew they crucified God's son?

2. What is forgiven when we are baptized?

3. What is baptism copying?

4. Which promise to Abraham are we a part of when we are baptized?

By Channah

72

Chapter 16

After the book of Acts, some of the books of the New Testament are letters written by the Apostles to the Christians in Jesus' Church in the places the Apostles traveled. Those books have the teaching in them on how to live after we become Christians. In fact, the names of the books have the names of the people in those places as titles. For example, Romans to the people in Rome, Philippians to the people in Philippi, Galatians to the people in Galatia and so on. The other books of the New Testament are named after the men who wrote them. For example, Timothy, Peter, James, etc. Remember II Timothy 3:16 the CEV Bible says, "everything in the scriptures is God's Word." God helped all who wrote the Bible to write just what He wanted us to know.

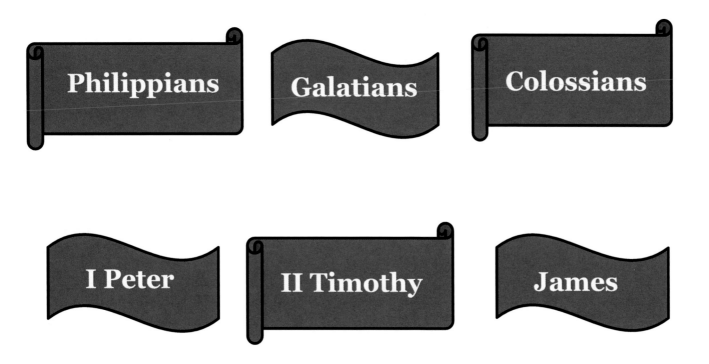

After we are baptized Romans 8:1 says, "Therefore there is now no condemnation for those who are in Christ Jesus." In I John 5:13 it says, "I write these things to you who believe in the name of the Son of God so that you may know that you have eternal life."

In I Corinthians 6:19-20 it says, "Do you not know that your bodies are temples of the Holy Spirit, who is in you, whom you have received from God? You are not your own; you were bought at a price. Therefore honor God with your bodies."

In the books the Apostles wrote to the Christians in the New Testament, they teach all about how we are to live. Everyone has different temptations in this life. We all have certain things that tempt us when others may have other things. When we become Christians, God is the only one that can help us fight against our temptations. The sins that tempt us are the same sins that have been temptations for people since way back in Noah's time. In Ecclesiastes 1:9 the CEV Bible says, "Everything that happens has happened before; nothing is new, nothing under the sun."

Keep in mind, we will not get everything right in this life, we will all sin even after we are Christians. That's why Jesus died for us! That's why God's big plan to save us is so important. Having a weakness, doesn't make us bad people in God's eyes. In Hebrews 4:15 the Bible says, "For we do not have a high priest who is unable to empathize with our weaknesses, but we have one who has been tempted in every way, just as we are—yet He did not sin." In I John 1:9 the TPT Bible says, "But if we freely admit our sins when His light uncovers them, He will be faithful to forgive us every time. God is just to forgive us our sins because of Christ, and He will continue to cleanse us from all unrighteousness." In I Corinthians 10:13 the ESV Bible says, "No temptation has overtaken you that is not common to man. God is faithful, and He will not let you be tempted beyond your ability, but with the temptation He will also provide the way of escape, that you may be able to endure it."

One of the ways we can get guidance from God is by talking to Him. We talk to God by praying. You can pray anytime or anywhere. You just tell Him all of your battles, thoughts, worries, fears, and what you are thankful for and soon He will become your closest friend and Father. Philippians 4:6-7 says, "Do not be anxious about anything, but in every situation, by prayer and petition, with thanksgiving, present your requests to God. And the peace of God, which transcends all understanding, will guard your hearts and your minds in Christ Jesus." We pray to God through Jesus name, so at the end of whatever you want to tell God, you may say, In Jesus Name, Amen. In John 14:13-14 the ESV Bible (Jesus is talking) says, "Whatever you ask in My name, this I will do, that the Father may be glorified in the Son. If you ask Me anything in My name, I will do it." Just remember some things we ask God for may not be the best for us at the time or you may have to wait awhile. Remember God knows what our futures hold too. In Romans 8:28 the NAS Bible says, "And we know that God causes all things to work together for good to those who love God, to those who are called according to His purpose."

Another way we can get guidance and help from God is by reading our Bible as it is God's words to us. Any subject you want to know about, you can type the subject in your phones and ask for all the Bible scripture on that subject.

Please keep all of these things in mind as you read the following verses of things we **all should not do** and things we **all should do** in our Christian lives.

A few of the verses that tell of the things we should not do are in I Corinthians 6:9-11, which says, "Do you not know that the wicked will not inherit the kingdom of God? Do not be deceived: Neither the sexually immoral nor idolaters nor adulterers nor male prostitutes nor homosexual offenders nor thieves nor the greedy nor drunkards nor slanderers nor swindlers will inherit the kingdom of God. **And that is what some of you <u>were</u>**. But you were washed, you were sanctified, you were justified in the name of the Lord Jesus Christ and by the Spirit of our God". Ephesians 5:1-10 and Colossians 3:5-10 also list what we should not do as Christians. I encourage you to look these verses up and read them for yourselves.

Now I want to give you a few of the verses that tell of the attitudes God wants us to have. In Galatians 5:22-23 says, "but the fruit of the Spirit is love, joy, peace, patience, kindness, goodness, faithfulness, gentleness, and self-control. Then Philippians 4:4-8 says, "Rejoice in the Lord always. I will say it again: Rejoice! Let your gentleness be evident to all. The Lord is near. Do not be anxious about anything, but in everything, by prayer and petition, with thanksgiving, present your requests to God. And the peace of God, which transcends all understanding, will guard your hearts and your minds in Christ Jesus. Finally, brothers, keep your minds on whatever is true, pure, right, holy, friendly, and proper. Don't ever stop thinking about what is truly worthwhile and worthy of praise."

Faithfulness   **Self Control**   **Gentleness**   **Love**

Joy   *PATIENCE*   PEACE   **Goodness**   **Kindness**

Knowledge Check

1. Who did the Apostles write books to in the New Testament?

2. What do those books teach us as Christians?

By Isaac

76

Chapter 17

Our story does not stop here! Before Jesus went back to Heaven to live, He told His Apostles what to look forward to. In John 14:1-3 Jesus said, "Do not let your hearts be troubled. Trust in God; trust also in Me. In My Father's house are many rooms; if it were not so, I would have told you. I am going there to prepare a place for you. And if I go and prepare a place for you, I will come back and take you to be with Me that you also may be where I am." In Acts 1:9-11 it says, "After He said this, He was taken up before their very eyes, and a cloud hid Him from their sight. They were looking intently up into the sky as He was going, when suddenly two men dressed in white stood beside them. "Men of Galilee," they said. "why do you stand here looking into the sky? This same Jesus, who has been taken from you into heaven, will come back in the same way you have seen Him go into heaven."

Philippians 3:14, 17-21, the CEV Bible says, "I press on toward the goal to win the prize for which God has called me heavenward in Christ Jesus......My friends, I want you to follow my example and learn from others who closely follow the example we set for you. I often warned you that many people are living as enemies of the cross of Christ. And now with tears in my eyes, I warn you again that they are headed for hell! ......But we are citizens of heaven and are eagerly waiting for our Savior to come from there. Our Lord Jesus Christ has power over everything, and He will make these poor bodies of ours like His own glorious body."

This is what will happen when Jesus comes back for the saved people! I Thessalonians 4:16-17 says, "For the Lord Himself will come down from heaven, with a loud command, with the voice of the archangel and with the trumpet call of God, and the dead in Christ will rise first. After that, we who are still alive and are left will be caught up together with them in the clouds to meet the Lord in the air. And so we will be with the Lord forever. " Hebrews 9:27-28 says, "Just as man is destined to die once, and after that to face judgment, so Christ was sacrificed once to take away the sins of many people; and He will appear a second time, not to bear sin, but to bring salvation to those who are waiting for Him."

Now let's take a look into what Heaven may be like! In Revelation 21:3-21 and 22:3-5 the CEV says, ".....God will make His home among His people. He will wipe all tears from their eyes, and there will be no more death, suffering, crying, or pain. These things of the past are gone forever. The glory of God made the city bright. It was dazzling and crystal clear like a precious Jasper stone. The city had a high and thick wall......The wall was built of jasper, and the city was made of pure gold, clear as crystal. Each of the twelve foundations was a precious stone. They were, jasper, sapphire, agate, emerald, onyx carnelian, chrysolite, beryl, topaz, chrysoprase, jacinth, and amethyst. Each of the twelve gates was a solid pearl. The streets of the city were made of pure gold, clear as crystal..... He and the Lamb will be seated there on Their thrones, and it's people will worship God and will see Him face to face. God's name will be written on the foreheads of the people. Never again will night appear, and no one who lives there will ever need a lamp or the sun. The Lord God will be their light, and they will rule forever." What a wonderful place to look forward to!

In the meantime, the Bible tells us to keep meeting together as a Church. Acts 2:42 says, "They devoted themselves to the apostles' teaching and to the fellowship, to breaking of bread and to prayer." The breaking of bread is the Lord's supper. I Corinthians 11:24-26 says, "He took bread, and when He had given thanks, He broke it and said, "This is My body, which is for you; do this in remembrance of Me." In the same way, after supper He took the cup, saying, "This cup is the new covenant in My blood; do this, whenever you drink it, in remembrance of Me." For whenever you eat this bread and drink this cup, you proclaim the Lord's death until He comes." Acts 20:7 says, "On the first day of the week we came together to break bread. Paul spoke to the people and, because he intended to leave the next day, kept on talking until midnight." Ephesians 5:19 says, "Speak to one another in Psalms, hymns and spiritual songs. Sing and make melody in your heart to the Lord." I Corinthians 16:2 says, "On the first day of every week, each one of you should set aside a sum of money in keeping with his income, saving it up, so that when I come no collections will have to be made." Hebrews 10:23-25 says, "...And let us consider how we may spur one another on toward love and good deeds. Let us not give up meeting together, as some are in the habit of doing, but let us encourage one another—and all the more as you see the Day approaching.

All of these things the Bible is talking about is how we worship together. It says, on the first day of the week, they were taught, ate the Lord's supper, prayed and sang songs to each other and gave of their money. This is how we worship God and continue to encourage each other until Jesus comes back to take us to heaven!

After we are baptized, we wait for Jesus to come back to earth to take all of us to Heaven to live forever and ever! Revelation 1:6-8 says, "Look! He is coming with the clouds. Everyone will see Him, even the ones who stuck a sword through Him. All People on earth will weep because of Him. Yes, it will happen! Amen. The Lord God says, "I am Alpha and Omega, the one who is and was and is coming. I am God All-Powerful!"

As long as we choose to become Christians and continue to try to live like Jesus, then Romans 8:37-39 says, "..In all these things we are more than conquerors through Him who loved us. For I am convinced that neither death nor life, neither angels nor demons, neither the present nor the future, nor any powers, neither height nor depth, nor anything else in all creation, will be able to separate us from the love of God that is in Christ Jesus our Lord."

Psalm 139:1-14 says, " You have looked deep into my heart, Lord, and You know all about me. You know when I am resting or when I am working, and from heaven You discover my thoughts.

You notice everything I do and everywhere I go. Before I even speak a word, You know what I will say, and with Your powerful arm You protect me from every side. I can't understand all of this! Such wonderful knowledge is far above me.

Where could I go to escape from Your Spirit or from Your sight? If I were to climb up to the highest heavens, You would be there. If I were to dig down to the world of the dead You would also be there.

Suppose I had wings like the dawning day and flew across the ocean. Even then Your powerful arm would guide and protect me. Or suppose I said, "I'll hide in the dark until night comes to cover me over." But You see in the dark because daylight and dark are all the same to You.

You are the one who put me together inside my mother's body, and I praise You because of the wonderful way You created me. Everything You do is marvelous! Of this I have no doubt."

I can honestly tell you there really is a God and He's crazy about you! We read that He even knows how many hairs are on your head! We never have to feel alone or afraid because when you become a Christian, God's Spirit is in you and He goes everywhere with you. God's love for us is so strong! John 3:16 says, "God loved the people of this world so much that He gave His only Son, so that everyone who has faith in Him will have eternal life and never really die." God gave His only Son to take our punishment for our sins on the cross. God is an amazing Father to us and will never leave us. Jesus blood makes us pure and holy and righteous. God did all of this because He wants us with Him in heaven forever.

Thank you God, for loving us so much and for your wonderful plan for Jesus!!
In Jesus name, Amen.

The End?

No!

Just the Beginning!

Knowledge Check

1. Before Jesus went back to heaven, what did He promise His apostles He would do?

2. Who did Jesus promise He would come back to earth for?

3. From the Bible's description of heaven, what do you think heaven will be like?

4. When we meet together as a Church, what are the things we are to do to encourage each other?

5. After we are Christians and are trying to live like Jesus, can anything separate us from the love of God?

Answer Key to Knowledge Check

Chapter 1

1. If we choose to have faith in God, how can we make our faith stronger? **Studying God's Word**

2. What book can we read about God that actually has His words in it? **The Bible**

Chapter 2

1. After God made everything , who was the first man and woman He made? **Adam and Eve**

2. Where did Adam and Eve live? **The Garden of Eden**

3. The devil talked Eve into sinning. What was the first sin? **Eating from the tree of knowledge of good and evil**

4. Who did God plan to send to save us from our sins? **Jesus**

Chapter 3

1. Whose ancestors was God protecting throughout the Old Testament of the Bible? **Jesus**

2. Why did God want to destroy everyone on earth? **Because they were being so sinful**

3. Whose family loved God and was kept safe during the flood? **Noah's**

4. Which of Noah's sons was Jesus coming from? **Shem**

Chapter 4

1. Who was Shem's great, great grandchild? **Abraham**

2. What were the **three promises** God made to Abraham? **1. The huge family 2. The land of Canaan 3. All people would be blessed through Abraham**

3. Who was going to be the blessing for all people? **Jesus**

Chapter 5

1. Who was the son God promised to Abraham and Sarah? **Isaac**

2. When Isaac married what were his twin son's names? **Jacob and Esau**

3. Which twin son was Jesus coming from? **Jacob**

4. To start the huge family promise, how many children did Jacob have? **12 sons**

5. Which one of the 12 children was Jesus coming from? **Judah**

Chapter 6

1. Why was Joseph's brothers jealous of him? **Their father gave him a special coat**

2. What was the first thing the brothers did to get rid of Joseph? **Put him in a well**

3. What was the second thing they did to Joseph? **Sold him to men going to Egypt**

4. Was Joseph used in God's plan to bring Jesus? **Yes**

5. Which brother was Jesus coming from? **Judah**

Chapter 7

1. Who told Pharaoh what his dream meant? **Joseph**

2. What did his dream mean? **There would be 7 years of plenty and 7 years of famine**

3. After Joseph was put in charge, who came asking for food? **His brothers**

4. Pharaoh told Joseph's family to stay in Egypt and while they were there which Promise came true? **The 1st promise of the huge family**

5. Which one of Joseph's brothers was Jesus coming from? **Judah**

Chapter 8

1. When Egypt had a new Pharaoh, why didn't he like the Israelites? **He was afraid they would take over his land**

2. What horrible thing did Pharaoh do to try and stop the Israelites family from getting bigger? **Kill all the boy babies**

3. Who did God save in this story to use in His plan to bring Jesus? **Moses**

4. Who is Jesus coming from in the Israelites? **Judah**

Chapter 9

1. What did God tell Moses and Aron to ask Pharaoh? **To let God's people go**

2. What were some of the things God did to make Pharaoh want to let His people go? **Turn their water to blood, frogs, gnats, flies, grasshoppers, sores on their bodies, hail, death of the firstborn**

3. Did Pharaoh ever let God's people go? **Yes**

4. Who was Jesus coming from in the Israelites? **Judah**

Chapter 10

1. When the Israelites left Egypt, what did God do when they came to the Red Sea? **Parted it**

2. When Pharaoh's Army came after them and tried to cross the Red Sea, what did God do? **He made the sea go back together and drown the army**

3. After the Israelites long travels what land did God give them? **Canaan the promised land**

4. What Promise came true in this story? **The 2nd promise, land of Canaan**

5. Which Israelite was Jesus coming from? **Judah**

Chapter 11

1. After the Israelites were living in Canaan, what did they pester God to give them? **Kings**

2. What was one of their good King's name? **David**

3. Who did he marry? **Bathsheba**

4. Who was Jesus mother Mary and earthly father, Joseph, coming from? **David and Bathsheba's children Nathan and Solomon**

Chapter 12

1. What plan can be traced through the entire Bible? **God's plan to bring Jesus to save us**

2. Who came to tell Mary she was going to have baby Jesus? **An Angel**

3. What town was Jesus born in? **Bethlehem**

4. Who told the shepherds about Jesus being born? **An Angel**

5. Which promise is coming true because Jesus is born? **The 3rd promise, all people would be blessed through Abraham**

Chapter 13

1. When Jesus was a man, who baptized Him? **John the Baptist**

2. What did God say when He came up out of the water? **This is my Son whom I love, with Him I am well pleased**

3. After Jesus was baptized what did He go around doing? **Teaching and healing people**

4. How many men did Jesus choose to help Him teach the people? **Twelve**

5. When Jesus sent the apostles to teach, what were some of the instructions He gave them? **Heal the sick, raise the dead, don't take any extra clothes, don't be afraid**

Chapter 14

1. Some people didn't believe that Jesus was God's son, what did they do to Him? **Crucified Him**

2. What things happened when Jesus was crucified that made the people realize He was God's son? **Darkness, an earthquake**

3. Who took our punishment for our sin on Himself? **Jesus**

4. What happened after Jesus was in the tomb for three days? **He raised to life**

5. According to what Jesus told the apostles, what will happen to anyone who believes and is baptized? **They will be saved**

Chapter 15

1. What did Peter tell the people they should do after they knew they crucified God's son? **Feel sorry for what they did, believe in Jesus and be baptized**

2. What is forgiven when we are baptized? **Our sins**

3. What is baptism copying? **Jesus death, burial, and resurrection**

Chapter 16

1. Who did the Apostles write books to in the New Testament? **The Christians**

2. What do those books teach us as Christians? **How to live our Christian life like Jesus**

Chapter 17

1. Before Jesus went back to heaven, what did He promise His apostles He would do? **Come back**

2. Who did Jesus promise He would come back to earth for? **The saved people**

3. From the Bible's description of heaven, what do you think heaven will be like?

4. When we meet together as a Church, what things are we to do to worship God and encourage each other? **Sing, preach, pray, take the Lord's supper, and give of our income**

5. After we are baptized Christians and are trying to live like Jesus, can anything separate us from the love of God? **No**

Credits

Redemption through Christ, Planned, Prophesied and Fulfilled by Rita G. Draper

New International Version Bible: many of the verses I've used throughout this book are from this version of the Bible, which is directly translated from the original Hebrew and Greek manuscripts. If the scripture does not say otherwise, it will be from this version.

Contemporary English Version Bible: Written as an easier to understand version, I've used several verses from this book to better make my point.

The Passion Translation Bible: The verses I used from this version will be marked.

The English Standard Version Bible: The verses I used from this version will be marked.

The New American Standard Version Bible: The verses I used from this version will be marked.

Children's Art: I have used my grandchildren's art throughout this book as chapter markers, with their permission of course.

Cloud Photo Page 78: Photo taken and submitted by R. Cherie Lepeak

Made in the USA
Monee, IL
07 July 2021